P6.

Mrs Abbott.

9.48.

£3

# THE VIKINGS

*Sledge found in Oseberg long-ship,*
*excavated in 1904 (Norway)*
*Silver beaker from Zealand, Denmark*

# THE VIKINGS

S. C. GEORGE

DAVID & CHARLES : NEWTON ABBOT

0 7153 6297 6

Set in 13/14pt Bembo
and printed in Great Britain
by Billing & Son Ltd Guildford
for David & Charles (Holdings) Limited
South Devon House  Newton Abbot  Devon

# CONTENTS

*England after the Peace of Wedmore (878), showing the Danelaw, where Guthrum's followers were allowed to settle. Ireland at that time was divided into seven major kingdoms.*

# *1*

# *THE VIKINGS*

Between the ninth and eleventh centuries bands of ferocious pagan warriors swept down with fire and sword from the cold, mysterious countries of Scandinavia upon the coasts of western Europe. Their dragon and snake-prowed long-ships created such terror that many churches added an extra prayer to the litany: 'From the fury of the Northmen, may the good God deliver us.' It was even believed that they cooked their victory feasts in cauldrons upon the bodies of their victims.

These warriors became known as 'vikings'. Some came from Norway, some from Denmark, some from Sweden. At times they combined against their enemies. Often they fought each other, even their fellow-countrymen.

Raids had occurred over a long period, but in the eighth century an outburst of great viking raids marked the beginning of the so-called 'Viking Age', an age which only began to draw to an end when Harald Hardrada's army was routed by Harold of England in 1066.

The vikings were first of all warriors and the most ferocious pirates ever known, yet they loved poetry and the telling of tales. Adam of Bremen, who wrote about them in the eleventh century, said that in peacetime Norwegian vikings lived off their livestock, using milk for food and wool for clothing.

Their main pursuits were trading, agriculture, cattle-breeding, hunting, fishing, carting dried fish and making charcoal.

In the fever of battle vikings fought with terrifying strength. Sometimes they bit the rims of their shields in their rage. Such men came to be known as *berserks*, a word probably derived from *bare-sark* (shirtless), because they discarded their armour in order to fight more freely. The expression 'to go beserk' is still used to describe a mad violence during which a person seems to feel no pain. The condition seems similar to 'running *amok*' (or 'running amuck') when a man loses control of himself and strikes down anyone in his path. *Njal's Saga* describes one such berserk, who feared neither fire nor sword, and all dreaded his arrival.

The men took their weapons and jumped on to the benches to await his approach. The berserk came rushing fully armed into

*Head of the wooden stem-post of a viking ship found in a river in Belgium. 4th–5th cent*

the hall; he strode at once through the fire . . . He brandished his sword to strike at the benches, but the sword caught in a crossbeam as he swung it upwards.

And this incident ends with the statement that the men fell upon him and killed him. Another name applied to these fighters was 'wolf-coats': 'the berserks roared in the midst of battle, the wolf-coats howled and shook the iron (spears)', says an old story.

The origin of the word 'viking' is uncertain. At least a century before England was attacked by vikings, the word *wicing* (a warrior) was in use; it corresponded to the Old Norse word *vikingr*, which Danes applied to pirates. In the late viking period, Greeks called them *baranggoi*, derived from the Old Norse word *vaeringjar*, which applied to the Varangian Guard, a famous band of warriors. The vikings were great traders and it is interesting to note that the Greek word originally meant 'an agent able to offer security in trading transactions'. Then there is the word *vik*, meaning a creek, inlet or bay, and one leading authority, the late Professor Brøndsted, declared, 'A viking was a pirate who lay hidden in fjord, creek or bay, waiting to pounce upon passing vessels.' It has also been argued that 'viking' comes from the Old English word *wic*, a camp, or the Norse word *wikan*, a seal, as the vikings were skilful seal hunters. To go *i-viking* was their own usual term for a combined trading and plundering expedition across the sea.

Not a lot is known about the vikings before the ninth century. The ancient Scandinavian tales, the sagas, were told from generation to generation until they began to be written down about the beginning of the twelfth century. These stories tell of courage, cruelty, treachery, easily affronted honour, blood feuds, ruthless ambition and constantly changing alliances between men and groups of men, and between the three countries of Norway, Sweden and Denmark. They tell also of loyalty, of dangerous journeys into unknown seas, of past history as known and imagined, of the way men and women loved and lived, of the beginnings of law and order, and of the widespread belief in gods, giants, dwarfs and witchcraft as well as of the coming of Christianity.

Story-tellers, or sagamen, and Icelandic poets were popular and held in high honour at feasts. No kingly court in Scandinavia was complete without a poet to glorify his patron and immortalise him in stirring verse. The highest compliment a viking could receive was to be called a great seafarer. The praise was doubly welcome if paid before his fellows, for the viking was seldom modest. And because a great man gained yet more honour from the mighty deeds of his ancestors, their exploits, too, were embroidered into the stories. When they were told, witnesses of the related incidents were often present, so although exploits might well be over-praised and even exaggerated they could not be wildly distorted. There is far more truth in the sagas than was once supposed, and events mentioned in them are confirmed by discoveries made by archaeologists. In 1962, for example, they found the site of Greenland's first little Christian church set up by the wife of Eric the Red.

Story-tellers were popular in lonely farm and great hall alike, for what better entertainment could there be on a long, icy, Scandinavian night than to hear how one's ancestors were carried in the long-ships over creaming seas to unknown lands, with no guide but the sun by day and the Pole Star by night, or driven by wind and current no one knew whither.

Various reasons have been advanced for the wide-ranging expeditions of the Viking Age. Perhaps the lands could no longer support populations swollen by the common practice of polygamy. Or if may be that, unable to live by cattle-raising and agriculture, the younger sons of landowning chiefs (who were not heirs to their father's property), as well as fierce men in disfavour with their rulers, were eager to embrace the more exciting and profitable trade of piracy. They would have no trouble in collecting crews of fighting-men, especially from the lower classes, many of whom were on the verge of starvation owing to crop failures. And there was another cause: trade was increasing everywhere as populations rose. The Arabs had won control of the western Mediterranean and alternative trade routes had been found. One of the most important ran across the south of Jutland, enabling ships to reach the Baltic from the North Sea without having to pass the dangerous Skaw to the north. This made it particularly attractive to the Danes. The Rhine, too, had become a great thoroughfare, and the North Sea coasts offered many opportunities for trading.

The control of trade routes was obtained by force. Vikings scorned death; they were brave and resolute, and thirsted for glory in battle. Trade and piracy went hand in hand. There was rich plunder to be had, and slaves to be seized for work in the homelands and for sale abroad. Coasts poorly defended because of internal quarrels, like those of England and Ireland, were a constant temptation.

The vikings' early attacks on the rest of Europe were uncoordinated and lacking in method. Later they began to seize islands in rivers and to occupy them as bases. Their first raids were generally made during the summer. If they wintered anywhere, it was likely they would try to settle.

Bede's old monastery at Jarrow, fifty miles down the coast from the holy island of Lindisfarne had been raided in 793 and was attacked in 794. Here the raiders were beaten off by Northumbrian fighting men who captured one of their chiefs and flung him into a pit of adders, possibly as a sacrificial offering. But the viking appetite was keen, and marauding ships began to sweep down England's eastern seaboard as far as Weymouth, leaving behind a trail of devastation.

In 795 the vikings seized an island in Dublin Bay. Over a period of twenty years they established themselves on all the

Irish coasts except the eastern one. Scotland, too, suffered, and on the Continent every navigable river was soon infested with vikings. From Byzantium, or Constantinople—the modern Istanbul in Turkey—to the Mediterranean coast of Spain, and from the Black Sea to the Baltic, the vikings fought their way, and began to accept Christianity at the same time as they plundered its churches. While western Europe was being ravaged, Russia was being founded by other vikings.

They formed colonies and set up their own kings in England, Scotland and Ireland, and in the lands of the Franks and Slavs. They colonised Greenland, Iceland and the Faroe Islands, and even tried, unsuccessfully, to colonise North America, 500 years before Columbus.

Wherever they settled they left place-names and words. Many of these survive in the English language and in local dialects today. Lincolnshire was a centre of Danish colonisation, and as a boy I played on a Horncastle field called The Wong. *Wong* was the Danish word for one of the blocks or strips of land into which an open field was split up for ploughing. Place names ending in -by and -thorpe, meaning village, are Danish word endings. Yorkshire's 'Ridings' derive from an Old Norse word meaning a third part. Many Old English words were supplanted by Scandinavian words; some of those in use are 'sky', 'take', 'knife', 'leg', and 'egg'.

The vikings enriched the language, influenced the literature of Europe with their poetry and left behind many splendid examples of their art. But in some respects they looked to other countries for their needs. In the latter part of the viking period they obtained from the Franks much better iron weapons than they could manufacture themselves. Their best glass was also imported. The trefoil brooch worn by Scandinavian women was of Frankish origin, and many designs of their goldsmiths and silversmiths probably originated from Baltic countries. They cut up beautiful art treasures in precious metals to pay for their purchases. Though they minted coins, they had very little use for them. The basis for their best military engineering came from the world outside their own. Their runic alphabet was invented by Germanic peoples hundreds of years before the viking period, and few vikings understood it. Their rich decorative art with its grotesque animal motifs was stimulated by contacts with foreigners. It took them 300 years to learn to build in stone and brick after their pagan gods had been toppled by Christianity. When they became colonisers, as in Normandy and England, they ceased to be vikings, and became part of the mixture of races from which the modern Frenchman and Englishman descended.

# 2

# A WAY OF LIFE

Despite what the story-books say, pirates never made their victims walk the plank, and vikings never fought in helmets with attachments such as horns or wings. The Oseberg tapestry shows a figure wearing what looks like a horned helmet and a few other similar representations have been found, but such helmets were worn only on ceremonial occasions.

A viking helmet was conical in shape and made of iron or leather. Metal helmets may have been a luxury of the rich; one of the few that have been found had attached to it a heavy eye-guard and nose-guard. Another found in Gotland was encrusted with copper and silver and had a decorated nose-guard. Some that have been discovered bear the small crest of a boar, an animal linked with the goddess Freyja who had protective powers.

The viking's favourite weapons were his sword and axe. The two-edged iron sword had a blade some 90 cm long and a hilt often richly chased and gilded, or inlaid with gold, copper and silver. Some swords were said to have been made by the dwarfs, or given by the god Odin. From his sword and long-handled, broad-edged battle-axe, a viking was never separated. He also had either a throwing-spear or a thrusting-spear, and a long, simple kind of bow; arrows were carried in a cylindrical quiver.

*Tapestry from Oseberg long-ship—reconstruction. Leading the procession in the tapestry is a viking wearing a ceremonial helmet with horns attached. Such representations are extremely rare.*

*Viking helmet from Norway. Despite popular tradition there were no horns or wings on battle helmets*

*Swords found at Windsor, Norfolk and Nottingham*
*The two-edged iron sword was a favourite viking weapon*

*Weapons, chain-mail, part of a helmet and other armour (Norway)*

*Axes threaded on to a stave of spruce (Denmark)*

An iron knife hung at his belt. His wooden shield was flat and round with an iron boss and was sometimes painted. A viking named his weapons and armour as he did his ships. *Snake of the Attack* was the name of a spear, *Bird of the Sling* of an arrow, *Ice of Battle* of a sword, while the famous Harald Hardrada named his *byrnie* (coat of ring-mail) *Emma*.

Those who could afford it wore chain-mail over a shirt and under-breeches of wool or linen; others had a thick, woollen, belted coat with long sleeves fitting neatly at the waist and reaching half way down the thigh. A tunic was worn over the shirt, red and leaf-green being popular colours. There were two kinds of trousers; one wide and baggy which may have been worn by the rich, the other kind narrow and tight. A long cloak, with two points almost touching the ground, was also worn. Hose were held to the leg with bands. Gloves and mittens of wool and fur were also in use. Vikings delighted in silver-bound swords and jewels, gold bracelets, scarlet cloaks and rich ornamentation. In *Njal's Saga* a chieftain is described as wearing

a blue tunic with a silver belt, blue-striped trousers and black top-boots. He was carrying a small round shield, and the axe with which he had killed Thrain Sigfusson and which he called *Battle Troll*. His hair was combed well back and held in place by a silk head-band.

17

(left) *Chain-mail shirt found in a burial mound (Norway). These were worn by the wealthier warriors*
(centre) *Silver pendant in the form of a man's head, found in Sweden. 10th cent. The vikings delighted in jewellery and ornamentation*
(right) *Viking gold ring found at Hamsey churchyard, Sussex, England*

The head-band was often richly worked in elaborate designs with gold thread. Woollen cuffs covered with silk and embroidered with gold thread were another adornment. When a viking's loot included rich brocades and silks from the East he must have cut a splendid figure.

Viking women of means wore a head-dress like a cap, shoes of tanned leather, and a long, flowing, sleeveless dress over a fine chemise. The dress had straps from which two oval brooches of bronze hung on the breast. Her scissors, keys and similar objects used in housework dangled from light chains around her neck. Her hair was knotted at the back. Young unmarried girls

*Necklace found at Halton Moor, Lancashire*

*Hoard of arm-rings found in Sweden. The spiral ones are from eastern Europe*

sometimes wore a short skirt and long boots and kept their hair loose. Brooches, rings and dress fastenings were popular. Slaves might wear only a blanket with a hole in it slipped over the head like a *poncho*.

Houses did not conform to any one pattern, but depended upon the kind of building material available. Where there was no timber, they were built of stone, clay and turf. A site excavated in Gotland revealed the foundations of a house about 19 m by 8 m. The double walls had been made of logs with

19

(left) *Necklace of silver filigree beads and pendants from Sweden*
(right) *Necklace with charms and arm ring from a grave at Birka, Sweden*

wattle-and-daub between them. Another rectangular house had its wooden walls faced with turf. Several methods of building with wood were used, such as making walls with vertically-set staves or planks. The big, smoky halls were the preserves of the rich, where guests were welcome in the long winters. At the beginning of the viking period peasants had to be content with living in one cold, smoky and smelly room of a single long-house, which they shared with their cattle.

Most of the people worked on farms or on the sea, and many had to contend with semi-starvation, cold and sickness. As the viking period progressed and wealth began to flow into Scandinavia, so conditions improved. A barn and store-houses would be added, and the barn homestead, with buildings surrounding a square yard, was eventually adopted. In Norway a site was found of a building some 24 m long by 18 m wide. Its wooden walls packed with clay had been built on a stone foundation, and the roof had been supported on inner posts. When building in the Orkneys and Shetlands, the vikings made dry-stone walls of natural flat stones. A house some 30 m by 8 m has still to be excavated at Westness in Orkney. In the Hebrides, stones from the fields and blocks of lava were used; in Greenland, stones and in grazing lands of Atlantic islands, turf. In Iceland a new pattern emerged; added to the long-house were lobby, kitchen, scullery, bathroom and sometimes a guest-room. The foundations of one Icelandic long-house were 36 m long; it had been built with slightly curved turf walls and with a fireplace in the centre of the hall. In a Greenland house a stone conduit had carried water through from the back wall and out through the front. The same arrangement can be seen

(left) *Cavalry brooch from Gokstad long-ship*
(right) *Brooch found at Hunterston, Scotland*

(above) *Exterior view of a reconstruction of an Icelandic long-house, Trelleborg*

(below) *Interior view of reconstruction of the Trelleborg house*

in an old stone house in Culross, Fifeshire, where Danes had settled. This house also contained painted panels of decorated woodwork, as in Norwegian farmhouses, but most of this panelling was ripped out in recent times and was even used by villagers for the repair of hen-roosts.

Most long-houses were dark, with windows high up in the walls. It is thought that pigs' bladders may have been used for panes until glass was invented in the Middle Ages. Long-houses in the north-west of Scandinavia had no windows at all; their earthen floors were stamped down and often strewn with weeds. Chairs and tables were in use, with benches sometimes lining the walls. The central section of one bench where the house-owner sat was known as 'the high-seat', though it was no higher than the rest. Any guest he entertained sat opposite him. The high-seat was flanked by posts called the 'high pillars'. At night the benches served as beds. Cupboards were unknown, though chests were common. Tablecloths and knives were in use, but not forks.

*Domestic implements of birchwood from burial mound*
*(spoon, curved ladle, scoop, etc)*

*Rhineland pottery found at Birka, Sweden*

Fields were cultivated with the plough, sickle, scythe, spade and hoe. Domestic animals were the horse, which the viking loved, the ox, sheep, goat, pig, dog and cat. The method of extracting iron from bog-ore was known, and the most important craftsman was the blacksmith. Some of the richest graves discovered were those of iron workers. Furs and slaves were exported to other countries.

In early times, the vikings had no separate kingdoms, but there were many clans paying service to a chief. A group of chiefs might elect a king from among themselves. Only in later years did a king obtain his title by inheritance. Next in line came the earls, men powerful enough to claim this rank, and wealthy enough to have a company of servants and own ships. Below them were the peasantry, free men and smallholders; these were the backbone of Scandinavian society, whose main occupation was producing food. Lowest of all were the slaves,

*Horse collars from Sollested and Mammen*

25

*Tools from a craftsman's chest found in a lake in Sweden*

who had no rights at all and belonged body and soul to their masters. They performed all the heaviest and most unpleasant tasks. They were despised and considered cowardly, unreliable, dull-witted and almost untouchable.

Viking law was based upon the decisions of free men in an assembly known as *The Thing*. Its rules were jealously observed, and preserved for posterity by word of mouth. Money payments on an agreed scale were fixed as compensation for murder and acts of violence. The punishment most dreaded was banishment.

Death was despised and every viking accepted the risk of it in battle. The dead were buried or cremated. There were many sorts of burials: in coffins, in large wooden chambers, under great mounds, in flat fields or in boats. Ship burials under mounds, or barrows, with the prows pointing to the sea, were

*Tools from a grave at Bygland, Telemark*

common for chiefs, except in Denmark. If there was no ship, or if one could not be spared, stones would be arranged in the outline of one. Customs varied, but a ship burial may have been designed to let a man sail into the next world in his own vessel. Or he may simply have been buried in his boat so that his spirit would feel more comfortable in the grave. Rich objects were often left in the grave, perhaps as offerings to the gods, or perhaps for the use of the dead man in the next world.

# 3

# GODS, GIANTS AND DEMONS

The viking world was wild and fearful, filled with magic and superstition, peopled with wizards and witches. It was a world where malevolent spirits swarmed, and a man who rose from the dead would work harm unless he were killed again to give his spirit rest.

Scandinavians were pagans for the greater part of the Viking Age. Though they believed in another existence after death, spirits of the dead were thought to live in or about the burial mounds, keeping each other company. Yet there were other gloomy worlds; one for the dead presided over by the goddess Hel, and another of malicious giants and giantesses, such as Freyja who drove a chariot drawn by cats. The giants lived among desolate crags and mountains in earth's outer ring; also living among rocks were wise and cunning dwarfs, great craftsmen in metal. Both giants and dwarfs could be tricked or caught, or could be bargained with.

There were many major gods, minor gods and goddesses, and lesser divinities. The gods were divided into two tribes, the *Aesir* and the *Vanir*. Divine women, the valkyries, carried the souls of dead warriors to Odin's huge 640-roomed, silver-roofed

*Gods or heroes fighting monsters are depicted here on dies used for making embossed plaques (Sweden)*

hall in Valhalla in Asgard. Odin was the chief of the gods, and had an eight-legged horse, Sleipner. In Valhalla, the dead warriors were enrolled in the mighty army who would serve under the great god Odin at the Last Day when all created things come to an end in the final battle with the forces of evil.

The gods lived in a world of their own, meeting, talking, playing, quarrelling and fighting. They had splendid houses and possessions, but though they were mightier than man, they had his weaknesses, too. Odin's passion for learning drove him to indulge in deceit and treachery. He even gave one of his eyes for a draught of water from the spring of Mimir which gave wisdom and understanding. He was interested only in the powerful, in warriors, magicians and poets, ignoring the humble and the unassuming. He had favourites, but changed them often. He learned about happenings in the world from his ravens and the spirits of hanged men. Strangest of all, even those who worshipped him did not trust him to keep his word. He would bring unexpected death to a warrior in battle so that he could enrol him in his vast army in Valhalla.

Odin's eldest son was the great, red-bearded Thor. He had a wonderful hammer named Lightning, iron gloves and a goat-drawn carriage which made the thunder as it rumbled across the sky. He had, too, a magic belt which doubled his strength. Thor was often outwitted by the giants, the enemies of the gods, but in the end he always won. A more humane god than the others, Thor protected peasants, made the crops grow and was invoked at weddings.

Then there was Loki, half god, half devil, the son of one giantess and married to another. His children were dreadful monsters; one, the World Serpent, lived in the ocean in which the world floated; Fenri, the giant wolf, was vicious and cruel; the third, Hel, ruled over the land of death.

The one wise, kindly and merciful god was Baldr, whose

(left) *Statuette (c. 1000) of Thor, the god who protected peasants, made the crops grow and was invoked at weddings*
(right) *Bronze image of a god, probably Freyja, from Rallinge, Sodermanland*

mother had obtained a promise from plants, animals and rocks that they would not harm him. But she overlooked the mistletoe. Loki made a dart from it and persuaded Hoder, the blind god, to throw it at Loki, guiding his hand to do so. And, of course, Baldr was killed by it.

31

Thor was tricked into wrestling with the World Serpent which wrapped itself round the earth biting its own tail so that its grip could not be broken. Thor almost tore it loose, and the earth shook. Had he succeeded the earth would have fallen apart. On another occasion Thor was tricked into trying to drain a horn, one end of which, though he did not know it, was open and rested in the sea. He had to give up, but not before he had almost drained the sea dry.

In this strange and terrifying world, Yggdrasil, the tremendous ash-tree, pushes up its crown to the sky, flings its branches over the earth and projects its three roots, one down to the land of the dead, one into the land of the Aesir, and one into the land of the Frost Giants.

On the day of Ragnarok, horrors and dreadful deeds will abound. The wolf Fenri's slavering jaws will gape from earth to heaven. Yggdrasil will shake. Heimdal, watchman of the gods who could even hear wool growing on a sheep, will blow his horn from the flaming Rainbow bridge only the gods can cross, and at the sound of it dwarfs will cower and whimper. Then will begin the last battle between gods and monsters. All will be slain, and the sun will turn black, the stars and moon fall from the sky, and the sea engulf the earth. On this sea a crew of giants will sail in a ship made from the nails of dead men, and these too will be swallowed up. But there is still hope, for two gods without guilt, Baldr and blind Hoder, will return, the sinless will live again, the eagle will once more soar and the sun shine upon a new and better world.

These stories may be a way of showing a belief in life after death, and the final triumph of the forces of good over evil. It has also been suggested that the battle of Ragnarok describes in a picturesque way the birth of a new year when green things burgeon after the stark desolation of winter.

In the last third of the Viking Age, the old beliefs began to be eroded by Christianity, though missionaries had long

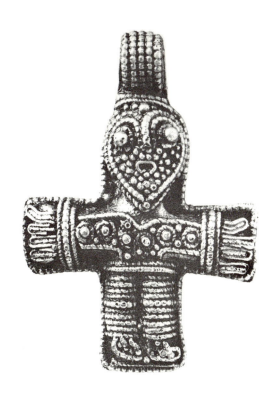

*The earliest known viking crucifix c.900 (Sweden)*

preached it and had made converts. Denmark was the first Scandinavian country to accept conversion. The Danes originally came into contact with Christianity on their trading expeditions, and perhaps found it easier to trade with Christian countries if they were Christians themselves. As early as 823, Archbishop Ebbo of Rheims was sent to convert Denmark, but only in the middle of the century was the first Christian church built, in the Danish trading centre of Hedeby. While many vikings admitted that Christ was a god, they declared that their own gods were greater. King Canute was an enthusiastic Christian, and though the new faith was strongly encouraged by the Danish kings, they did not force it upon the people.

*Smith's mould for casting amulets of the cross and Thor's hammer, a mixture of Christian and pagan superstition*

The first Christian king of Norway was Hakon the Good who had been educated by the Anglo-Saxon king, Aethelstan. Hakon took Christianity to Norway, but its people were finally terrorised into accepting it between 995 and 1030, by the cruel methods of Olaf Tryggvason and Olaf the Stout.

The first Christian mission to Sweden in 829 was led by Angsar, who was nearly killed by pirates on his way there. He was allowed to build a church in the trading centre of Birka, but Christianity did not prosper and at the beginning of the eleventh century the country was still completely pagan. By the twelfth century, Christianity was widely accepted, but for a long time thereafter, whenever things went wrong, the people turned again to their old gods. It had been a practice of slave-owners to expose at birth the unwanted babies of slaves as a a means of controlling the birth rate and so economising on household expenditure. When Christianity forbade the practice, slavery began to decline.

The fierce, independent, blood-feuding vikings could not have found it easy to accept a faith which preached submission, forgiveness and humility.

# 4

# THE LONG-SHIPS

The *Anglo-Saxon Chronicle* for the year 793 recorded that flying dragons and other terrifying sights were seen in England, and that famine followed. These things, declared the monks, were omens of the scourge that would punish people for their sins. In that year, Norwegian viking long-ships, with their snake-like prows apparently poised to strike, were beached on the defenceless little island of Lindisfarne off the Northumbrian coast. Fierce warriors leapt ashore, murdered the monks, plundered the gold and silver, burned down the church and monastery, and carried off the novices into slavery.

A ship was a viking's most treasured possession and the height of his technical skill. It was built for speed and mobility. At first the sail was only a square of cloth high up on the mast. Later a huge, magnificent, square sail, often striped, was used, and may have been copied from those on Roman galleys.

Some half-dozen long-ships have been found intact in great burial mounds, or 'barrows', by the sea's edge in Norway. Three of them are now in the viking ship museum at Byddø outside Oslo. One was discovered at Tune on the east side of Oslo Fjord in 1867; one at Gokstad, in a barrow near Sandefjord in 1880, and the third at Oseberg on the Oslo Fjord in 1903. These ships had been developed from early patterns, such as the

*A silver chalice from Jellinge*

one found at Nydam in South Jutland in Denmark. This was merely a large open rowing boat with a rudimentary keel, and without sail or mast.

The Tune ship had been robbed in ancient times. In it were the skeletons of a man and a horse buried in a standing position. Horses were used for mobility and dragging carts, and not in battle. The Gokstad ship, built about the year 800, was well preserved by the blue clay in which it was deeply buried. The Oseberg ship was also built about 800.

The only viking ship found in Denmark, in 1935, had been commissioned at the end of the ninth century during the reign of Harald Fairhair. It, too, had been pillaged. Robbers had reached it through a hole made in the chamber side and another hole in the ship itself. Inside the ship lay the skeleton of a chieftain, a powerfully built man, six feet tall, well-armed and well-dressed. Three rowing boats were stacked inside the prow; amidships were bronze and iron kitchen utensils, wooden spades, a carved sledge and a wooden gaming board. Outside the boat but inside the burial chamber were fragments of woollen cloth and silk embroidered with gold thread, the remains of a leather

*The Gokstad long-ship, built c. 800*

purse, an axe, buckles and mounts of lead, iron and bronze. Inside the mound, but outside the chamber, were some peacock bones and the remains of twelve horses and six dogs. The mound was 49 m long and 5 m high; the ship inside it was 23.3 m long, 5.25 m in the beam and 1.95 m deep from the gunwale to the bottom of the keel. Its dead weight would have been about 9 tons, and its draught not more than 90 to 95 cm. Amidships was a heavy block of oak, and above this another fish-tailed

*The Oseberg long-ship, built at approximately the same time*

block with a hole in the middle to support a mast. Along each black gunwale thirty-two shields were set, painted alternately black and yellow; each shield half covering the next. Shields were removed, of course, during voyages.

The blade-shaped steering-oar, a huge piece of oak just over 3 m long, was fastened to the starboard side of the ship by a stout riveted cleat. Through the cleat, the ship's side and rib, holes had been bored to take a tree-root or withy by which the

*A bed from the Gokstad ship*

steering-oar could be operated. Such a vessel could not sail into the wind. A tiller was in the neck of the rudder at a convenient height for the helmsman who stood on a rising poop. The pine mast was some 12 or 13 m long. The sail could have been red, blue, red-striped or chequered. There were sixteen pairs of 5-m oars; their blades passed through circular oar-holes which could be closed by wooden covers when the ships was under sail. The oarsmen had no thwarts; their sea-chests were probably fastened down and used as seats. A narrow plank about 7 m long served as a gangway. The Gokstad ship contained four planks with carved animal ends. These were probably gables for a tent when it was pitched ashore. There were eight beds in the ship, two with animal heads to guard the sleeper; there were also fragments of blankets and eiderdowns. The ship itself was built of oak, with decking, mast, yards and oars of pine.

The Oseberg ship contained the remains of two women, one of whom might have been Queen Asa, mother of King Halfdan the Black, and grandmother of King Harald Fairhair. The ship's

*The Oseberg ship being excavated (1904)*

gunwales at each end rose 5 m above the waterline. It is thought
that the ship was designed for luxury, and it may have been an
old vessel laid up and refitted for the funeral.

Along with such objects as wall-hangings, a loom, a barrel of
wild apples, various kinds of fruit and grain, sledges, tents, beds
and gang-planks, there was a four-wheeled wooden cart with
carved panels and long shafts. One of the carvings is of the
head of a Norwegian viking, a round-faced, low-browed man
with sweeping moustaches and carefully trimmed beard. He is a
completely different type from the short-haired, more finely-
featured Swedish viking carved on the top of a bone stick which
was found at Sigtuna.

The ships depended for their steering entirely upon the

oarsmen, of whom there were three shifts for long voyages. In a sixty-man vessel, twenty would be rowing and the other forty available for fighting. These shifts were necessary as ships could not anchor at night and, if there was no wind, rowing might have to be continuous.

The average ship seems to have had a crew of forty, chosen from volunteers after trials of strength, and for their skill at helm and oar, and with weapons. Strict regulations governed their conduct. Quarrelling aboard was forbidden; women were barred from warlike expeditions; all plunder was divided according to rule. Horses seized on raids were used only to transport warriors quickly from point to point.

As trade developed, cargoes were carried in broader, bulkier ships with their bulwarks built up so that goods could be stacked between them. All ships were designed with a shallow draught so that they could sail up rivers, and bore such names as *Elk of the Fjords* and *Raven of the Sea*.

As the Viking Age progressed, vessels became larger, perhaps twice the size of the Gokstad ship, though the design was the same. The biggest ships were called dragons because of the

*Sledge from the Oseberg ship*

41

*Wagon from the Oseberg ship*

carvings on their prows. One of the most famous, *The Long
Serpent*, built for King Olaf in 998, was 37 m long and had
thirty-four benches for rowers. The prow and stern were
covered with gilding. Up to that time it was the longest, finest
and most costly ship ever made in Norway.

Vikings had to navigate by rough and ready methods. On a
clear night they could not fail to see the two pointer stars in the
Great Bear constellation wheeling round the Pole Star. A
navigator could measure with the fingers of his outstretched
arm the Pole Star's distance above the horizon, allowing two
degrees of latitude for each finger. Of longitude he knew
nothing. The sun at noon standing at its highest pointed due
south. Sailors knew, too, how far from land the different species
of birds would travel at certain times of the year. How the
vikings managed to navigate when the sun was obscured is not
known, though King Olaf the Stout boasted that he had a
magic 'sun-stone', which told him where the sun was in cloudy

*Head of a norseman; carving on wagon found on the Oseberg ship*

43

(left) *Viking* head carved in elk-horn from the top of a
stick found at Sigtuna
(right) *Picture stone from Gotland, showing a viking ship*

conditions. It has been suggested that, if such stones were used,
they may have been either the crystal Icelandic spar or tourma-
lines, both of which have been found in viking burial mounds.
These stones are said to change colour when turned in polarised
light, and this would be sufficient for a viking to tell the
difference between east and west.

But how would a modern navigator like to sail by directions
such as were given in the Icelandic *Landnamabok*?

From Hernar in Norway you are to keep sailing west for Hvarf
in Greenland and then you will sail north of Shetland so that you
can first sight it in very clear weather, but south of the Faroes so
that the sea appears half-way up the mountain slopes, but to the
south of Iceland so that you may sight birds and whales from it.

# 5

# 'WARE THE VIKINGS

Norwegians landed on the treeless Shetland Islands, the Orkneys and the Hebrides at the end of the eighth century. Some of their towers, known as *brochs*, still exist. Probably intending to settle, they seized from the painted Picts land which soon became bases for attacks upon the mainlands of Ireland, Scotland and England.

Their task was made easy in Ireland by its internal quarrels. The vikings plundered freely and carried young men and women into slavery. Turgeis, or Thorgest, a notorious Norwegian chieftain, reached Ireland with a large fleet in 839. He forced the Norwegian settlers in Ulster to acknowledge him as their king, and dubbed himself 'King of all foreigners in Erin'. He seized Armagh, a great centre of Christianity in Ireland, tried to force the worship of Thor upon the Irish people, and allowed his ferocious wife to celebrate pagan rites on the high altar of the captured monastery of Clonmacnoise. Dublin, which he founded, soon became a popular port with Scandinavian traders and vikings.

Every spring the north-east winds blew the long-ships to Ireland where their crews wintered and later built permanent forts. It was only a matter of time before Danish vikings fought Norwegian vikings there. But the Danes were at last driven out, leaving the Norwegians to plunder as they pleased and establish strongholds and permanent bases at Waterford, Wexford, Limerick and Amagassan on the coast of Louth.

In 835, barred from Ireland, the Danes began to plan settlements in England. They started with a raid up the river Thames, deliberately spreading terror everywhere. Scarcely a church within a day's ride of the coast from the Humber to the Solent escaped them, and there are churches today which bear the marks of their burning. Danes driven from Ireland captured York. In Kent, they were bought off temporarily by the payment of *Danegeld* (Dane money), an extortion frequently repeated in later years, and one which always led to demands for more.

Ragnar Lodbrok's three sons made East Anglia the base for a united viking 'Great Army'. The kingdoms of Northumbria, Mercia and East Anglia were overthrown, but in Wessex, which was defended by King Aethelred and his brother Alfred, the vikings were checked. On 8 January 871, Alfred 'like a wild boar' led out his levies against them. The battle began without the king who was at mass and refused to leave until it was over. The result of the battle was indecisive, though the Danes were forced back into their camp at Reading with the loss of one of their kings and five nobles. A fortnight later Aethelred was defeated at Basing. Ten weeks later he died, and was succeeded by Alfred.

For a time Wessex was left alone while the vikings savaged Mercia and Northumbria. With York as their base, they began systematically to colonise. Then half the Danes in Northumbria turned again to Wessex after subduing East Anglia and Mercia. They had initial successes and were joined by fleets from France and Ireland, and also from Wales. The vikings had failed to establish themselves in Wales and, in fact, never secured a foothold there.

In 878 the vikings suffered their worst reverse when a hundred

*Birchwood bucket from Northumbria found at Birka, Sweden*

of their ships transporting their army were lost in a storm off the Dorset coast. Some survivors decided to settle in Mercia; the rest, reinforced by a fleet from Ireland, pressed Alfred so hard that he had to seek refuge 'in great sorrow and unrest' in the forests and swamps around the Isle of Athelney in Somerset. A host of legends gathered about his name, and in later days he loved to tell of his adventures there.

Just before Easter, the men of Devon broke out of a position where they were besieged, and routed a Danish army at the battle of the Raven Banner. This was the name of the famous standard supposed to have been woven by Ragnar Lodbrok's daughters between dawn and dusk of one day. The raven embroidered on it was said to flutter its wings if the army was advancing to victory, and to droop them if defeat was fated.

Contingents of English from the western shires met at a secret rendezvous on hills overlooking the Vale of Knoyle. Six weeks after Easter, to their great joy Alfred joined them. The opposing armies met at Edington, and during many hours of hard fighting with sword and axe the issue was doubtful. At last, advancing in single line behind walls of shields, the English broke the Danish ranks and drove the enemy in confusion towards Chippenham. Alfred pursued them vigorously, though his men could scarcely stand from fatigue. The Danish camp was fourteen miles away, the route marked by thousands of viking dead. Quantities of cattle and stores were captured, and after a fortnight's siege the dispirited Danes surrendered.

Alfred now earned his title of 'the Great', for he was generous to his enemies and victimised no one. By the Peace of Wedmore, in 878, Guthrum, one of three Danish kings with the Great Army, withdrew his claim to that part of Mercia south-west of Watling Street. Alfred agreed that the Danes could remain where they had settled beyond it. The area extended to the Humber and the Wash and centred around the 'Five Boroughs' of Lincoln, Stamford, Leicester, Nottingham and Derby. This land, which Guthrum parcelled out among those of his followers who wished to settle, was thereafter known as the Danelaw. At York Guthrum became the Danes' own Christian king, and many of his followers were baptised with him.

The Danes kept the terms of their agreement with Alfred until 886 when they broke out again. But Alfred had used the respite well, reorganising his army, fortifying boroughs and towns, and building ships. The *Anglo-Saxon Chronicle* under the year 896 says

Then King Alfred had long-ships built to oppose the Danish warships. They were almost twice as long as the others. Some had 60 oars, some more. They were both swifter, steadier and also higher than the others. They were built neither on the Frisian nor on the Danish pattern, but as it seemed to him himself that they could be most useful.

Alfred beat the Danes in various encounters and recaptured London from them, adding it to his kingdom of Wessex. Thereafter the Danes in England became part of the population and gave Alfred no more trouble. He had reorganised his defences so well that he was able to repel an attempted viking invasion launched from the Continent. Those vikings who did not return to Scandinavia settled peaceably in the Danelaw.

After Alfred died in 900, the overseas vikings left England alone for three-quarters of a century. In Ireland, too, the turning point came when Aed Findleath, high king from 862 to 879, forced the vikings to abandon all their bases in the north. Yet the Norwegian viking kings of Dublin were never more powerful than in the early years of this period. Not only did they wage war in England and Scotland, but they nearly seized control of all Ireland after a long struggle with the Danish vikings of Northumbria. Then, in 902, Cearbhall, King of Leinster, easily captured Dublin, slaughtered many vikings there, and drove the rest out of Ireland.

The Norwegian vikings elsewhere in Ireland struck back, and the Irish suffered blood-baths in various battles, especially at Islandbridge on the north bank of the Liffey. Here their high king, Niall Glundubb, and twelve Irish kings with him were slain. Soon Limerick was captured and held as a viking settlement, but the last viking prince in Ireland, Olaf Curran, King of Dublin, was later defeated and fled as a Christian pilgrim to Iona where he died, a broken man.

Of all who resisted the vikings, none, apart from Alfred the Great, could compare with Brian Boru, son of a Munster chieftain. In his youth he had fought the Danes until he had only fifteen men left, and he kept on fighting though his brother made peace. After many notable victories he became king of Cashel and the mightiest man in Munster, and was everywhere recognised as the high king of Ireland. In 1014, towards the end of his days, rebels and vikings plotted against him. A great army drawn from the Orkneys, the Hebrides, Cornwall, Wales, Normandy, Francia and Scandinavia, launched a desperate attack to preserve Dublin as a viking trading centre. Brian rallied Ireland around him, and one spring morning at the head of 20,000 men under seventy banners he faced the viking army at Clontarf where modern Dublin stands. Brian was slain, but by nightfall the viking army was routed; 7,000 rebels and vikings lay dead with 4,000 of the victorious Irish army. The vikings never regained their old power in Ireland, and gradually the stream of invaders dried up.

In Scotland, vikings from Ireland were pillaging during the first two decades of the tenth century. One of the great names in the viking history of Scotland is that of Thorfinn the Mighty, a cousin by marriage of Harald Hardrada's wife Thora. He seized the Orkneys and became lord of all the lands between the Orkneys and the north and west regions of Scotland. He had eight earldoms in Scotland and great estates in Ireland. The Isle of Man was also under him, and he was a formidable rival to the Scottish king.

The Master of Caithness and Sutherland was Thorstein the Red who built himself a fortress at the mouth of the Moray Firth. He was killed in a curious way by a dead Scottish chief whose head he had cut off and tied to his saddle. The chief had a tusk-like tooth which scratched Thorstein's leg as he rode along, and it set up an infection from which he died.

At the end of the century, Magnus Barefoot, King of Norway, seized the Orkneys, the Hebrides and the Isle of Man, but was killed in Ulster. The Isle of Man and the Western Isles maintained their loyalty to Norway through intrigues, quarrels and murders until 1266 when they were ceded to Scotland, after more than four hundred years of viking domination in western Scotland. Orkney's link with Norway lasted until 1468 when Christian I, King of Norway and Denmark, gave the islands to James III of Scotland as security for his daughter's dowry. The Shetlands were formally annexed by Scotland in 1272, nine years after the battle of Largs, which both sides claimed as a victory.

Meanwhile the Danes had again turned their attention to England. In 910 they were thoroughly routed in Mercia, and their fighting spirit was so broken that they suffered one defeat after another. Edward, eldest son of Alfred the Great, and his sister, Aethelfleda, were accordingly able to begin the conquest of the Danelaw. The Danes submitted after Guthrum, their king, was slain; they were allowed to keep their estates and live according to Danish law and custom. Pursuing his campaign, Edward forced Ragnvald, the Danish leader who had captured York, to conclude a hasty peace. Many Danes left England and joined the vikings on the Continent.

Edward was succeeded by his son Aethelstan who, in 927, conquered the whole of Northumbria and captured York. When the Scots and the Strathclyde Welsh rose, Aethelstan and Edmund, his young half-brother, accompanied by 300 vikings, marched north and joined battle with a great allied force of vikings in Dumfriesshire. They won a resounding victory, and the sorry survivors fled to Dublin.

England enjoyed twenty-five fairly quiet years up to 980, by which time she was a single realm from the Forth to the Channel. In 978, Aethelred the Redeless (the 'Ill-advised'), popularly known in later years as 'the Unready', had acceded to the throne at the tender age of ten. England once more suffered a nightmare of raids. Year after year Olaf Tryggvason ravaged the coasts, his ships manned mainly by Swedes from Russia. Time and again they were bought off with ever increasing payments of *Danegeld*. Aethelred committed his most outrageous act when, on St Brice's Day, 1002, he ordered the massacre of all Danes, peaceful or not; among the murdered was the sister of Swein Forkbeard, King of Denmark and Norway. The vikings revenged themselves ferociously. In one expedition the Archbishop of Canterbury was carried off and, after a substantial sum had been paid as *Danegeld*, the vikings, all drunk, pelted him with bones and ox heads, and finally split his skull with the back of an axe.

At the head of a great fleet, Swein Forkbeard, accompanied by his eighteen-year-old son, Canute, swept into the Humber to avenge his sister's murder, and the Danes of the Danelaw offered him the crown of England. Aethelred promptly fled overseas. But a few days later, in the early part of 1014, Swein died suddenly at Gainsborough, and Canute claimed the succession. At the time he was the Danish commander in southern England, but he was driven out of the country and

*King Canute and his wife Aelgifu presenting a cross on the altar of Newminster*

returned to Denmark to raise fresh forces for a decisive attack upon England.

Canute returned in 1015 with a powerful fleet, accompanied by his brother Harald. Edmund Ironside, Aethelred's son, who until his untimely death in 1016 was a national hero, put up a stout resistance. The final battle was fought at Assandun, or Ashingdon. At the most critical moment Edric of Mercia fled with all his followers; what had seemed certain victory for Edmund became a heavy defeat and 'all the nobility of England was there destroyed'. It was then agreed that Edmund should have Wessex, and Canute the rest of the country including London. A treaty had just been concluded when Edmund died at the age of twenty-five. Canute, four years younger, became king of England.

At the beginning of his reign Canute appeared to be a blood-thirsty and faithless tyrant. He arranged the murder of Edric, who had deserted to his side. He also had Edwy, brother of Edmund, murdered and, had he dared, he would have killed Edmund's children as well, but instead he sent them to Olaf, King of Sweden. Others, too, whom he distrusted, were conveniently disposed of.

As a foreign conqueror, Canute was not involved in the jealousies between the various English tribal kingdoms. In case of need, he could obtain all the soldiers he wanted from Scandinavia, but he preferred to rule over a people by winning their loyalty, not by crushing them. To this end he pursued an anti-Danish policy, though it was a ruthless one. He banished his first wife, Aelgifu, and her two sons, Harald and Sweyn, and married Emma of Normandy, the widow and second wife of Aethelred. In his first year he levied an enormous ransom of 10,500 pounds of silver from London and 72,000 pounds from the rest of the country. He used this money to send back to Denmark all his Danish ships and soldiers, except for the crews of forty ships who became his bodyguard.

Next he summoned a national assembly at Oxford, and pledged himself to observe the good laws of the English King Edgar. Soon afterwards, his brother, King Harald, died childless and in 1019 Canute went to Denmark to assume the throne and to take steps to prevent further viking raids against England. Upon his return to England, he outlawed a powerful viking, Thorkel the Tall, and appointed Godwin, Saxon Earl of Wessex, in his place. Realising that he had been imprudent, he went back to Denmark and effected a reconciliation. However, he had to agree that Thorkel should govern Denmark in his absence. Thorkel died in about 1024, thus relieving Canute temporarily of any threat to his supremacy.

It was not long before a bid for the control of Norway was made by Olaf the Stout (later Saint Olaf), one of Harald Fairhair's descendants, who expected to be attacked by Canute.

*Bronze-gilt weather vane from Soderala church, Halsingland, probably from a ship in Canute's fleet*

King Olaf made an alliance with the king of Sweden and they chose the year 1026 for a combined attack on Canute. They hoped that an estrangement between Canute and his brother-in-law, Earl Ulf, would enable them to attract Ulf to their side. Their fleet assembled at the mouth of the river Helge in eastern Skane, where Canute, with a powerful Anglo-Danish fleet, joined battle with them. The result, though indecisive in some ways, left Denmark free from further threats. But just after the battle, Canute had Ulf murdered, possibly because he suspected him of contemplated treachery.

In England, Canute persevered with his reforms and efforts to conciliate his old English enemies. Possibly for political reasons he had embraced Christianity. At first he was a Christian little more than in name, but as time passed he became devout, and he cultivated good relations with the church so that he could have their assistance in government. He also made a pilgrimage to Rome to atone for Ulf's murder. While there, he attended the crowning, by Pope John XIX, of Conrad II as emperor of Germany, with whom he made an alliance. From Rome he sent a letter to his English subjects promising justice to all and strongly recommending them to pay their church dues. Later in his life he arranged a diplomatic marriage between Conrad's son and his own daughter, Gunnhild.

The most important change Canute introduced was his division of England into great earldoms. This reduced the power and influence of the former kingdoms and helped Canute in his policy of setting up a central government. He appointed a body of secretaries who travelled with him on his journeys; they were perhaps the beginning of a permanent administrative staff. Canute also minted money with the help of Anglo-Saxon mintmasters and introduced the Anglo-Saxon penny to Northumberland.

When Canute had established his authority, he ruled England with a strong hand and wise head. During his reign the country

+ Vniuersa quae in seclo presenti humanis uidentur oculis cito de
ficiunt. quae uero superis locantur montibus. Amoenitate
uigent continua. in summi tonantis regmine aeternaliter
fixa manentia. & idcirco nobis inuicem filiis seculi studendum est. ut
operibus iustis. frui mereamur bonis caelestibus. semp uicturi cum an
gelis scis. Unde ego . CHUT . Anglorum rex. uenerabili archi epo. Ælfsta
no. positione coniugis ac regnę Æl   é. quoddam siluulę nemus concedo.
famosa insilua . ANDREDESPEALDE . qu    loco dicitur . HÆSELERSC. quatinus
dies habeat pprios cum omnib: Adse rite ptinentibus. absq; omni seruitute
terrena. postq; finem secularem cui cumq; sibi placeat heredi. in aeternam re
linquat hereditatem. Siquis hominum ut non optamus hoc nrm donum
  nquam puertere uel frangere satagit. a xpo maledicatur omnibusq; scis
  si meum      i ar    mortem congrua emendet satis factione. quod nrm con
  te regium deliquit decretum. Istis terminibus predictum angitur nemus.
Dis synd an dis senne lano gemæru to hæsel  isce. ærest and lang ppanlæges bupnan. ðð punan leages
meapee. of punan leages meapee. be holan beames meapee. of holan beames meapee spa onge pulte
to pylæge bupan ðisne sithdan to pam geate. of pam geate innan þæne sithop. and lano silhepes
innan þæne bpaðan bupnan. nider and lano bpaðan bupnan. be þæs apice biscopes meapee epe innan
þeapin leages bupnan. Scriptaest haec castula mille decurso. Anno. xviii. his testibus
concordantibus. quorum nomina inferius scribuntur ·                    (qado

+ Ego. CHUT. rex hoc donum uenerundo archi presule. Ælfstano. aeternaliter con
+ Ego. VULFSTANUS. Archi eps hanc regis munificentiam corroboro.
+ Ego. Ælfgyfu. regina. beneficium hoc pdicto archiepo. Adnomeorege impetraui.

| | | | |
|---|---|---|---|
| + Ego. Godpinus. eps | confirmaui. | + Ego. Durkil | dux. | tes tis. |
| + Ego. Ælfpius.. eps | assensussum. | + Ego. Godpine | dux. | tes tis. |
| + Ego. Ælmærus. eps. | concordaui. | + Ego. Sigeryd | minister | tes tis. |
| + Ego. Ælfsinus. eps. | corroboraui. | + Ego. Byrh | minister | tes tis. |
| + Ego. Byrhpoldus eps | contradidi. | + Ego. Ælf | prefectus | tel tis. |
| + Ego. Byrhpinus. eps | conclusi. | + Ego. Ædelricus. | tes tis | fidelis. |
| + Ego. Ælmær | abbas. | + Ego. Godpinus. | tes tis | fidelis. |
| + Ego. Ælfpig. | abbas. | + Eg. Ælfsinus. | tes tis | fidelis. |
| + Ego. Ælfric | abbas. | + Ego. Ælfricus. | tes tis | fidelis. |

*Grant made by King Canute to Aelfstan, Archbishop of Canterbury*

56

was free from disturbances. Denmark perhaps profited even more by her close contact with a far more civilised nation, and the acceptance of Christianity by the nations of the north was hastened by Denmark's link through Canute with England. Danes and Anglo-Saxons had strong ties of customs, religion, laws, language and blood, and the viking settlement in England strengthened the obstinacy and determination in the English character.

Henry of Huntingdon, a twelfth-century chronicler, first recorded the well-known story of Canute's rebuke to the courtiers who flattered him outrageously by saying that even the waves obeyed his command. He placed his throne on the sea verge and demonstrated that when he ordered the waves to advance no further they still lapped the royal feet.

Canute fully justified the title of 'the Great'. He submitted himself to the laws and to the regulations of his own household troops. He was a diplomat of no mean order. He was a great warrior. He made his kingdom of Denmark secure from attack, and for a time controlled the greater part of Norway. At some uncertain date he led an army into Scotland, and Malcolm, King of the Scots, acknowledged him as overlord. In England he brought order out of confusion, but after his death his empire soon fell apart. He died on 12 November 1035, in his fortieth year, and was buried at Winchester. His remains lie with those of Emma in one of the six chests which contain the bones and ashes of twelve Saxon saints and kings. The original chest bore the inscription: 'Here rests in this chest Queen Emma. She was first married to King Aethelred, and afterwards to King Canute: To the former she bare Edward, to the latter Hardicanute. She saw all these four kings wielding the sceptre, and thus was the wife and mother of English kings.' The present chest, made in the sixteenth century, contains the old one and also bears the words 'Canute and his Queen Emma, the fair maid of Normandy'.

# 6

# THE SCOURGE OF EUROPE

At the beginning of the Christian era the Romans found a great trading people, the Frisians, occupying the coastal lands between the river Scheldt and the Ems. At the end of the eighth century they became subject to Charles the Great (Charlemagne) who was extending his Frankish empire in the north up to the river Elbe.

As a defence against his aggression, Godfred, the Danish king, built a great earthwork barrier, now known as the *Danevirke*, 'stretching from the eastern bay called Ostersalt', according to Frankish annals, 'to the western ocean protecting the entire northern shore of the river Eider and having but a single gate for carriage and horses to travel to and fro'. The *Danevirke* also protected a new trade route which by-passed the perilous journey round Jutland. When Charles the Great died, his vast empire fell apart, and its defences were neglected. The vikings saw their opportunity, and twenty years after his death in 814, their raids began.

The Atlantic coast was the favourite hunting ground of the Norwegian raiders, who followed the Loire to reach the heart of France. Quentovic, where Calais now stands, and Dorestad in the centre of Holland were the two main trading posts on the North Sea coast. These were constantly threatened by Danes. A Danish fleet of several hundred ships sailed up the Elbe and ravaged Hamburg. A smaller fleet plundered up the Seine and attacked Paris. Both Danes and Norwegians seized island bases, such as Walcheren at the mouth of the Scheldt, Jeufosse in the Seine to the north-west of Paris, and the tidal island of Nourmoutier whose monastery was attacked so often that the monks abandoned it. Frisian dykes were damaged and 2,500 homesteads destroyed. The whole of Frisia was at the mercy of the Danes. A Danish fleet, fresh from attacking London, destroyed Quentovic.

One of the main scourges of the three new kingdoms of the Frankish empire was Ragnar Lodbrok. Having hanged 111 prisoners of a defeated army, he was bought off with 7,000 pounds of silver after plundering Paris. Plague struck his fleet on its way home from Denmark, and for a few years the Seine valley was free, but from their Nourmoutier base vikings pillaged the Loire valley and Aquitaine, Frisia and Britanny. After a long siege they captured Bordeaux. The Great Danish Fleet plundered the Rhine valley and elsewhere until another temporary peace was bought by the grant to them of Dorestad. Paris was seized, most of its churches destroyed, and many other towns were sacked. Time and again the vikings were bought off with huge sums of silver and gold.

One notable long-range expedition left behind it a trail of blood and destruction when its 150 ships sailed on to Spain. There they laid waste the neighbourhood of Corunna until men from the little kingdom of Asturias defeated them, drove them back to the coast and destroyed half their fleet. The remaining vikings rounded Cape Finisterre, pillaged the coast near Lisbon, sailed up the Guadalquivir, captured Seville, ranged far and wide and plundered such cities as Constantina, Cordoba and Moron. Then the Moors drove them back to the sea, taking many prisoners and thirty long-ships. This was the first time the vikings had fought Arabs, to whom the whole Spanish peninsula had fallen in 712.

After their defeat, the vikings sailed on a plundering expedition up the river Tinto, but fled when they heard that the redoubtable Arab emir, Abd-er-Rahman, had arrived in Seville. Further disasters struck them. A storm dispersed their fleet. Some ships were driven on to the African coast; the rest returned to the mouth of the Gironde, plundering on the way.

Another long-distance expedition by sixty-two long-ships passed the Straits of Gibraltar, put to flight a Moorish force in Morocco, raided the Balearic islands, plundered southern France, returned to winter and pillage in the Rhone valley, sailed to Italy in the spring after being defeated by Franks and attacked Pisa. They gained entrance to the town of Luna by a ruse. With swords concealed under their cloaks and carrying a coffin, they begged for Christian burial within the town walls for Hasting, their leader. Once inside, the 'dead' man proved very lively indeed, for he and the coffin-bearers held the gate with their swords until their companions had poured through. On their return voyage to the Seine, they landed near Gibraltar, fought six battles with the Moors, then sailed away and captured Pampluna before completing their journey.

The years 865–6 were bad ones for the Franks; the vikings were finally bought off with 4,000 pounds of silver and a plentiful supply of wine, and this time the Seine valley had peace for the next ten years.

In 866 Brittany was attacked by Hasting, and soon afterwards the Danes began to send for their families and settle in the country they controlled. Fighting and looting continued, and in 885 a great fleet of 700 ships and 40,000 men led by the Danish vikings Sigfrid and Orm invaded France. Paris, still an island town, was besieged for several weeks, but Odo, the Frankish king of the West, finally trapped the viking fleet, and the Danes had to haul their ships over dry land to reach the river above the town in order to escape. After this reverse, Paris was left alone.

Constant fighting reduced the vikings' Great Fleet to 250 ships. In 892, the Continent was afflicted with dreadful famine and pestilence, and Sigfrid, the commander in chief, set sail for England and was followed by Hasting's vikings who had been defeated in Picardy.

The Danish army in Normandy spent several years fighting in the Seine valley. Rollo, their leader, acquired such a firm grip on Normandy that in 911 he was given a dukedom in return for his promise to the Frankish king that he would protect Normandy from further viking attacks. Apart from one or two small raids, Rollo kept his word. His followers settled down and became good Normans. Duke Rollo was said to be the only viking whose memory was treasured in a conquered land. Under him, Scandinavian law ended; the duke and his chiefs exercised complete power, and Normandy was the best-governed province in France.

Sweden became an organised kingdom long before Denmark and Norway. With the island of Gotland as a base, Swedes established themselves in parts of Latvia and Estonia. By way of the Gulf of Finland they reached Lakes Ladoga and Onega, and on the southern shores of Lake Ladoga, where Leningrad now stands, they founded a small colony named Aldeigjuborg (now Staraya). There they bartered furs, fish, amber, walrus ivory, honey and slaves, receiving in exchange wheat, wine and other goods which came along the trade routes from the East and elsewhere. Russia was divided into two empires, the Khazar in the south and the Bulgar in the north. By pushing forward their trade, the Swedes linked these two cultures.

From their new colony, by following the great rivers and their tributaries, often having to drag their ships over dry land, the Swedes reached the Black Sea where Greek colonies had been established, and from there Constantinople itself. Another trade route led to the White Sea and the trading centre of Byelosersk. A third route passed through the Bulgar empire and the Khazar empire—though a strong, armed escort was needed—to the Caspian Sea. After crossing the Caspian Sea they could travel along the established caravan route to Baghdad. The river Volga was later to become the vikings' first trans-Russian waterway and the most important trade route of Swedish and Gotland merchants. The river Dnieper route was disliked because Swedish settlers denied even their own countrymen free passage along it to the south. Arabs first met Swedes along these routes, and an Arab writer described them as bold and handsome barbarians, dressed in dirty clothes and wearing gold armlets, their only occupations being fighting and bargaining, their only merchandise skins and slaves. The men, he wrote, were big and ruddy and wore cloaks, and every man carried an axe, knife and sword. Their women wore brooches and chains around their necks, and they paid high prices for glass beads. They were 'the dirtiest people that God ever made'.

These colonists became known as the Rus, from which Russia may have taken its name. About the year 860, the tribes of the region around Lake Ladoga invited three brothers from Scandinavia to rule over them. Rurik, the most famous of the three, was an experienced raider in western Europe. In 862 he carved out for himself a princedom in Novgorod and founded a dynasty which lasted for 700 years. Oleg, his successor, founded the great Kievan state of which Kiev was the centre, and this is where Russian history began.

The Rus warriors, of whom Rurik was a leader, were called Varangians. Among their many exploits they attacked Constantinople to protect the Russian-Byzantine trade upon which Kiev's prosperity depended. Several attacks were made upon Constantinople. The third was led by Igor, son of Rurik, who chose a time when the Greek defenders were weakened by wars

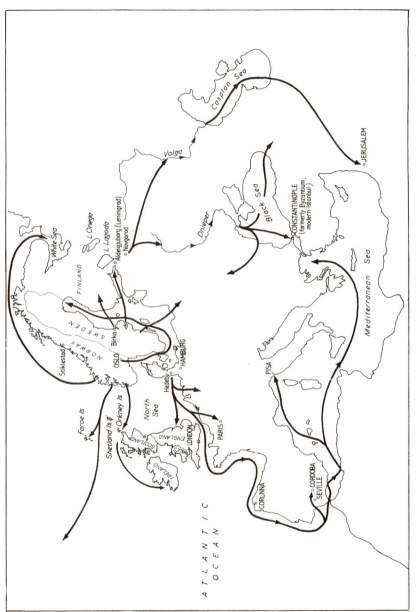

*The vikings in Europe: the Norwegians raided the Atlantic coast, the Danes plundered in France and the Swedes opened up trade routes to Russia.*

with the Saracens. The Greeks had only fifteen broken old galleys available, but these were well furnished with 'Greek fire', which was probably a mixture of such materials as quicklime, sulphur and naphtha. These ingredients were packed in a wooden tube cased with bronze. This container, called the siphon, was 'fired' by applying the hose of a water-engine to its breach. It was, in fact, a primitive flame-thrower. Wind and current were in the right direction. The flame-ships bore down upon the viking fleet whose crews watched their approach with contemptuous amusement, but when the fire was projected they were thrown into panic. Thousands leapt overboard to escape burning, and those who reached the shore were slaughtered by peasants and soldiers. About a third of the viking ships escaped, and Igor attacked again the following year. Once more 'Greek fire' was used against him, but this time, when it was spent, the Greeks were surrounded. They were compelled to buy peace by the payment of three pounds' weight of gold for every soldier and sailor in the Varangian fleet. Time and again the Varangians were bought off. They were a nuisance in Russia, too, until Vladimir I of Moscow finally persuaded them to seek a wealthier master—the emperor of Constantinople. They attended him, Gibbon says in his *Decline and Fall of the Roman Empire,*

> to the temple, the senate and the hippodrome; he slept and feasted under their trusty guard, and the keys of the palace, the treasury and the capital were held by the firm and faithful hands of the Varangians.

In the eleventh century, their strength was constantly recruited from the English and Danes fleeing from the yoke of William, England's Norman conqueror. Varangians even attacked Athens; a marble lion with a Swedish rune carved upon it was found in Piraeus harbour.

*Marble lion, with a Swedish rune carved on it, found in Piraeus harbour. (It is now in Venice)*

The two great Russian waterways for trade which Swedish vikings fought to control remained the rivers Dnieper and Volga. The Swedes sailed down the Volga to trade with White Bulgars and Khazars, and drove south along it into the land around the Caspian Sea. In 880 they seized a town in its south-eastern corner, but they were all slain by Moorish levies. On another raid on the coast of Persia, every man on their sixteen ships was killed.

Independent Swedish settlers had maintained their hold on the Dnieper route throughout the ninth and tenth centuries, and newcomers, vikings or not, were forced to take the Volga route. In the eleventh century, the two Rus districts of Novgorod and Kiev combined to form a Christian, West Russian Empire, and because Baghdad's production of silver fell off after their mines had been seized by eastern invaders, the importance of the Volga diminished, and the Dnieper became the Swedes' main trade route to the Black Sea and Byzantium. Later, during the Crusades, eastern goods were brought direct across Europe instead of by the Russian rivers and, when eastern nomads began to raid the west, the Dnieper route became more dangerous.

Trade was the reason for Swedish incursions into Russia, unlike the plundering, conquest and settlement of Danish vikings in England and France. But the Swedes often had to fight for control of the trade routes, and at times viking garrisons held such towns as Novgorod, Kiev and Smolensk. By the end of the viking period, their trade routes across Russia to the east had been abandoned, and gradually the settlers lost their identity and became Slavs.

# 7

# EXPLORERS AND
# SETTLERS

Not all the long-ships sailed to war-torn, western Europe. Some discovered the desolate shores of empty lands pounded by cold Atlantic seas. Northmen probably reached the Faroe Islands, only 200 miles from the Shetlands, when blown off course by storms. Round about the year 700, Irish hermits in frail boats, seeking escape from violence and searching for a hermitage, had found their perilous way to the Faroes where they lived in huts and caves until driven from their solitude by settlers from Norway.

The Icelandic *Landnamabok*, sometimes called the Book of Settlements, gives two versions of the discovery of Iceland in about 860. The first says that it was found by a viking named Naddod who was driven off course on a voyage from Norway; the other that Gardar Svafarsson, a Swede, made his home at a place called Husavik (House Creek) on a steep cliff overlooking a bad harbour. In the following spring he sailed round the island, leaving behind a crew member named Nattfari, together with a slave and a bondswoman.

The third settler in Iceland was Floki, who carried livestock with him and built his hall on the far side of Breidafjord. The site provided good pasture for his beasts, islands for their summer grazing and a fjord rich in fish, seals and birds. But when winter smothered his land in snow, and spring packed the fjord with drift ice, his livestock and his means of subsistence vanished. At the end of a long, bad season, the disillusioned Floki put to sea, but gales drove him back again, and he had to survive another winter before he could return to Norway. During this journey the cable to his tow-boat parted. The boat carried one of his companions, Herjolf, who was lucky to reach land safely. Another companion, Thorolf, reported well on Iceland, stating that butter dripped from every blade of grass, and was thereafter known as Thorolf Butter.

Several more voyages seem to have been made to Iceland, but there were no serious attempts at settlement until about the last quarter of the ninth century in the time of Harald Fairhair. Ingolf and Leif, having paid blood money for the murder of two brothers, decided to seek land and sanctuary outside their own country. While Ingolf equipped a ship, Leif sailed to Ireland for a last raid and returned with a sword and ten prisoners. With crews and the prisoners, the two ships left Norway.

Ingolf was the first to sight land. Following an old custom he flung overboard his high-seat pillars, the wooden beams which framed the seat of honour of the master of the house. These pillars, which symbolised the home, were thought to have magic properties. Wherever they were washed up, Ingolf and his crew would make their home; but he could not find them. Leif's pillars were washed ashore sixty miles away, and there he and his men settled. As Leif had only one ox, he made his slaves drag the plough. The slaves plotted together, slew the ox and told Leif it had been killed by a bear. When Leif and his followers entered a forest after the bear, the slaves murdered them, then sailed off with the women and all they could carry, and settled in a group of islands to the south-west.

Meanwhile Ingolf sent two slaves along the coast to search for his seat pillars. They found Leif's body and returned for Ingolf. Having buried his brother, he looked around and noticed some islands. Guessing that this was the hiding place of the murderers he sailed after them, surprised them at a meal and slew all except those who jumped to their deaths off a steep cliff in a desperate effort to escape. Ingolf took the women back with him. During his third winter in Iceland he found his high-seat pillars where the capital, Reykjavik, now stands, and there he built his house.

The settlement Ingolf founded was completed some sixty years later. Then came Eric the Red, who was to become famous in Greenland; Ketel Gufa with a gang of bloodthirsty Irish slaves; Grim who was said to have fished up a merman who prophesied his death before the next spring; and many others.

By 930 all the habitable area was occupied; only one-sixth of the land could support human life. Yet Iceland became a home for adventurous men who for various reasons had lost their land in Norway, or were fleeing from the tyranny of Harald Fairhair.

The Norse colonists arrived in sturdy ships carrying twenty to thirty men; women, children and slaves; animals, food and timber. Like Ingolf before them, many threw overboard their high-seat pillars and settled where fate or the gods decided. Skullagrim Kveldulfsson, whose dying father had said he would show him where to land, threw the coffin overboard instead of the high-seat pillars and built homes for himself and his followers where it drifted in.

In the main, the farming settlers never adapted themselves to local conditions, and within 300 years soil erosion was to cause most of the farms to be abandoned. The year 975 was marked by a terrible famine. The chronicles reported that

Men ate ravens and foxes, and many abominable things were eaten which ought not to be eaten, and some had the old and helpless killed and thrown over the cliffs. Many starved to death, while others took to theft, and for that were convicted and slain.

Harald Fairhair made laws to curb the power of settlers. No man could own more land than he and his crew could carry fire around in one day. A fire had to be lit at sunrise, then further smoke fires, so that each might be seen from the other. The first fires must burn until nightfall. A woman was not allowed to take in settlement more land than a two-year-old heifer could be walked round on a spring day between sunrise and sunset. The *Landnamabok* also stated:

This was the beginning of the heathen laws that men should not have a ship with a figurehead at sea, but if they did, they must remove the head before sighting land, and must not sail it with gaping head and yawning jaws lest the spirits of the land grew frightened of them.

Civil war raged as the land became useless. In the thirteenth century Iceland submitted to King Hakon of Norway and lost its independence. At the beginning of the fourteenth century, plagues, epidemics, starvation and earthquakes overwhelmed the people; farms vanished, and birds fell dead as they flew over the poisoned land after Mount Hekla, looked upon as the Mouth of Hell itself, had violently erupted. Yet Iceland somehow managed to survive.

Christianity came to Iceland during the reign, from 995 to 1000, of Olaf Tryggvason, King of Norway. Olaf believed in force as a means of conversion. According to the saga, he 'invited every man to accept Christianity; and those who opposed him he punished severely, killing some, mutilating others, and driving some into banishment'.

Olaf chose as his instrument a quarrelsome robber, Thangbrand, who had fallen into disgrace because of his frauds and piracies whilst a priest on a Norwegian island. Thangbrand's brawls often ended in bloodshed. As a punishment, Olaf sent him to Iceland, where he toured the country evangelising. He met a pagan farmer named Thorkal, who challenged him to a duel after a quarrel over religion. Thangbrand defended himself with a crucifix instead of a shield, and with it killed his opponent. Upon his return to Norway he told Olaf of the bad treatment he had received, and said that the Icelanders were so steeped in sorcery 'that the earth had burst open under his horse and had swallowed it'. Olaf was so angry that he would have had all the Icelanders in Norway put to death but for the intercession of two chieftains, Gizur the White and Hjalti, who offered to go surety for their countrymen and preach Christianity in Iceland. In 1000, Christianity was adopted as the religion of the commonwealth by the Althing, the Icelandic parliament which prepared the code of laws and the constitution, convoked national assemblies and continued to meet until the year 1798.

For a long time, however, many of those who accepted Christianity still worshipped the old gods in secret, like one Helge the Lean, of whom it was said, 'He was very mixed in his beliefs; he believed in Christ, and yet made vows to Thor for sea-voyages and in tight corners, and for everything which struck him as of real importance'.

Early in the tenth century, Gunnbjörn Ulfsson, sailing from Norway to Iceland, suffered the common misfortune of being blown off course, and he may have sighted Greenland's icy mountains. He made a landfall on some desert islands, afterwards named Gunnbjörn Skerries, but not until Eric the Red sailed to see if Gunnbjörn's skerries were habitable was the mainland of Greenland discovered.

Because of a feud ending in manslaughter, Eric, red-headed, red-bearded and red-handed, and his father, Thorvald, had been compelled to leave their farm in Norway. Unable to find land in Iceland, Eric, after sailing 450 miles, had landed on the southern extremity of Greenland's most habitable region, a beautiful place of flowery slopes overlooking a bird-haunted archipelago. He found traces of earlier occupation—probably Eskimo—and lived there for three years before returning to Norway. There had not been a single casualty among his followers.

Eric had named the country Greenland, hoping to make people more ready to go to a place with so pleasant a name. In north-west Europe, 976 had been a year of famine. Norway and England in particular had suffered. When Eric returned to Greenland it was as leader of a fleet of twenty-five ships. Some were wrecked on the voyage, others had to turn back, but fourteen arrived safely. About 400 people, mostly Icelanders, settled along the inner reaches of some 120 miles of the fjords. They formed the so-called Eastern Settlement, on the site of the modern Julianehaab district, which eventually contained 190 farms, a cathedral, a monastery and twelve parish churches. Several adventurous people travelled north for 300 miles to form the Western Settlement, where Godthaab stands today. It had ninety farms and four churches. Eric's farm at Brattahlid, protected by low hills with green pastures beside a sparkling stream, was discovered and excavated in recent times.

Overseas trading was vital to the settlers, for corn, timber and iron were in short supply. In exchange for these, and for weapons, clothes of Continental style, malt, wine and church vestments, exports were made of furs, Greenland woollens, hides, seal oil, ropes, cables, and ivory of walrus and narwhal.

The colonists soon discovered that Greenland did not live up to its name, The interior was covered by an enormous sheet of ice which had buried mountains and valleys far beneath its surface. The climate changed rapidly from bright sunshine to dense fog or heavy snow and arctic winds. In the thirteenth

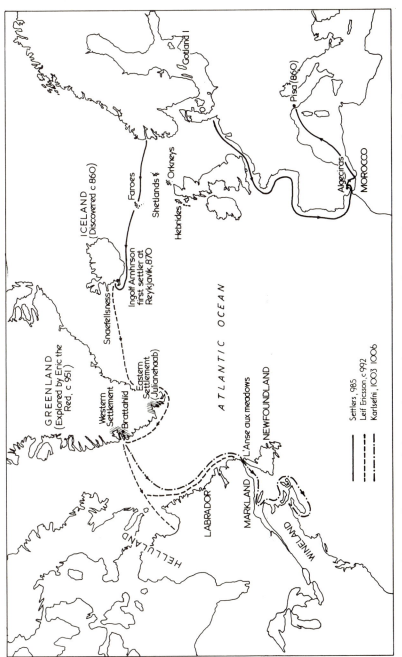

*Viking exploration of the northern Atlantic coasts, showing the routes taken by Leif Ericsson and Thorfinn Karlsefni.*

century the climate deteriorated; drift ice piled into the fjords, and the harvests diminished. As seals followed the ice south, the settlers went hunting for food and driftwood further north; Eskimoes following the seals must have clashed with the Northmen. The Norse population never exceeded 3,000. In 1261, the Greenlanders accepted the rule of the king of Norway, who forbade them to use ships so as to preserve the trade for Norwegians. A succession of cold winters and bad summers added to the miseries of the Greenlanders. By 1342 the Western Settlement had been abandoned. In some years of the fourteenth century no ships at all reached Greenland. After 1377, no bishop set foot in the country and Christianity died out.

The fate of the last of these early settlers is a mystery. There is evidence of the ravages of an epidemic soon after 1500. Also many inhabitants were carried off by the English as slaves. What happened to the last man? Did he die alone of sickness or starvation? Was he killed by Eskimoes? Or did he die by his own hand to escape the terror of loneliness in the world's greatest island?

# 8

# THE DISCOVERY OF WINELAND

Soon after the year 986, a young trader, Bjarni Herjolfson, sailed from Iceland for Greenland. It was his custom to pass the winter there with his father, who had a farm in the colony established by Eric the Red on the west coast.

Bad weather drove Bjarni in his trading ship blindly to the south-west, far off course. At last unknown coasts, low-lying and covered with forest, were sighted; possibly it was the Cape Cod peninsula they saw, certainly not Greenland. Bjarni kept on sailing in these unknown seas. Land faded from view, then again was sighted, still low and green and forested. It has been suggested that this was the south of Nova Scotia. Bjarni may then have sailed north; for the third time he sighted land, a cold country of mountains and glaciers, possibly Newfoundland. The crew had been anxious to land to obtain fresh water, but Bjarni, realising that this was not Greenland and anxious to find his bearings, sailed on for three more days. At last, after turning into the open sea, he reached Greenland where he was reunited with his father.

Bjarni's adventure was widely discussed. The new lands seen by him and his crew aroused speculation among vikings everywhere. It was some fifteen years before Leif Ericsson (son of Eric the Red), described in the *Greenland Saga* as 'big and strong, of striking appearance, shrewd, and in every respect a temperate, fair-dealing man', decided to visit the land which Bjarni had found by chance. If it should seem worth while he would explore and exploit it. Another version of the saga states that he was sent by Olaf Tryggvason of Norway to carry Christianity to Greenland, and like Bjarni was blown off course.

There was no reason why a ship which had weathered the journey once should not do so again. Leif bought Bjarni's ship and set sail with a crew of thirty-five. The sagas tell how he first found a land barren and ice-capped which he called Helluland, land of flat stones. Sailing on, he reached another low-lying wooded land with a good sandy beach which he named Markland, land of woods. Two more days' sailing brought him to land which may have been Labrador. It had a mild climate and wild grapes flourished. There were grassy, undulating hills, forests of mighty trees and meadows rich in wild wheat. There was an abundance of game ashore and of salmon in the rivers. Leif passed the winter there, then returned to Greenland, where he spent the rest of his days honoured by his fellows.

He called the country Vinland, or Wineland, because of its grapes. From the position where Leif said the sun rose on the shortest day, and because in America the vine does not grow further north than latitude forty-five degrees, it is not unlikely that Leif's Wineland was Maryland or Virginia.

The way had been shown and other voyages followed. Leif's brother, Thorvald, announced that he meant to explore the new country, and Leif gave him his ship and provided a crew of thirty. Thorvald reached Wineland safely, found Leif's old camp, and began to explore the country around it, but the only evidence of human life was a deserted wigwam. In the autumn he went back to Leif's camp, and when summer returned began

First reference ever to 'Winland' (line 7) from MSS of Adam of Bremen
in Caravel book c. 1180

exploring again. On the coast, hiding under a boat, they found nine Indians, whom they called *skraelings*. They killed eight; the ninth escaped, and that same night returned with a large war party. Thorvald and his men defended themselves behind their boat, and the Indians at last withdrew, having expended all their spears and arrows. Thorvald had been mortally wounded by an arrow which passed between the gunwale and his shield. He ordered his men to bury him on the pleasant headland where he had wanted to build his house. 'Bury me there,' he said, 'with a cross at my head and one at my feet, and let the place be called Crossness hereafter'. Thorvald was thus the first European to be buried in America. His men stayed until the following spring—the year was 1007—and then returned to Greenland with a cargo of grapes.

Then Thorstein, Thorvald's brother, decided to bring back the body from Wineland. He put to sea from Greenland in the same ship with a crew of twenty-five, but they were blown off course by gales. After sailing blind in storms for many weeks, and through fog and rain, they were driven back to Greenland and abandoned their plans.

Some years passed before another voyage was made to Wineland. Then, about 1020, Thorfinn Karlsefni, a rich Icelandic merchant, fitted out a vessel for trading to Greenland. Another boat joined him, and the two captains and their crews wintered in Greenland with Eric the Red. Karlsefni there married Gudrid, Thorstein's lovely widow. The feast that Christmas was the richest ever given there, and they enjoyed the winter, telling stories, feasting and playing draughts and chess with pieces carved from walrus ivory and whalebone. During this time Karlsefni and a friend named Snorri decided to lead another expedition to Wineland, intending to profit by it. They were joined by an Icelandic boat commanded by Bjarni Grimolfsson and Thorhall Gamlason, and a third ship, which Thorbjorn Vifilsson, the son of a war captive, had brought from Iceland. This was commanded by Thorvard, a Greenlander, who brought along his wife, Freydis, daughter of Eric the Red. With them was Thorhall the Hunter, an old man reputed to be bad-tempered, cunning and taciturn. He was huge, swarthy and uncouth. As he was usually abusive when he spoke he was unpopular, and he was also a trouble-maker. Altogether there were 160 people, most of them Greenlanders.

They first sailed to the Western Settlement of Greenland, then on to Bear Island. From there they voyaged south until they reached a country littered with boulders and great slabs of stone, from which they concluded that it was Leif's Helluland. Two days' sailing south brought them to a thickly wooded land which they assumed was Markland. Still farther south they reached a cape where they found the keel of a ship, perhaps one abandoned by an earlier Scandinavian explorer, and named the place Keelness. Then they journeyed past the bleak, sandy shores of Labrador, which they named Wonderstrands because it took so long to pass them. They put ashore two slaves from Scotland, a man named Haki and his wife Hekja, who had been given to Karlsefni for the expedition 'for they could run faster than deer'. These two were instructed to run and explore the land and return within three days. They bounded away dressed only in open-sided garments with hoods attached, fastened between the legs with a loop and button. Upon their return, one was carrying grapes and the other wild wheat, and they reported they had found good land.

The little fleet then continued south and put into a beautiful bay which they named Straumfjord, or Firth of Currents. Here they made their camp, and at first life was pleasant. There was a river with so many birds on it 'that one could scarcely set foot between their eggs' and plenty of grass for their cattle.

During this first autumn, Thorvard's son, Snorrie, was born, the first European to be born in America. The winter was severe and the hunting a failure. Accordingly the explorers moved to an island at the mouth of Straumfjord. Though their cattle thrived, they themselves continued short of food and 'prayed to God to send them something to eat, but God was not as prompt as they would have liked'.

Then Thorhall the Hunter, a man of unsettled mind, disappeared. A search party found him after three days behaving as though out of his wits. When he became normal he began to abuse them as rudely as ever. Soon after they had taken him back to camp, they killed and cooked a stranded whale. Thorhall, a pagan, claimed that it was sent to them by the god Thor in answer to his prayers. Some of the vikings were already ill after eating the whale meat, and when the rest heard what Thorhall had said they threw the remainder of the whale over the cliffs.

A little later, the weather broke, and they could fish again. When spring returned they hunted successfully and found plenty of eggs on the island. But Thorhall grew even more objectionable. He said that they were looking for Wineland in the wrong direction, and that he was tired of hard work, shortage of food and the failure to provide him with wine as promised. So, with nine others, he left the expedition, setting sail in one of the ships, only to be beaten off course by fierce head winds and driven on to the Irish coast. There he and his men were tortured and enslaved, and Thorhall died miserably.

Karlsefni and his people sailed south and reached a river which flowed into a lake and from the lake into the sea. Sandbars blocked the mouth of the river at low tide. Karlsefni named the place Hop, the word for an inlet, creek or tidal lake. This could have been the mouth of the Hudson river, or an island in the estuary of the St Lawrence. Here they dug pits in which they trapped halibut when the tide ebbed. The streams ran with fish, game was plentiful; wild wheat waved on the low land, and vines sprawled on the higher slopes. Their surviving cattle had good pasture, so they decided to settle there.

A fortnight later, nine canoes appeared, full of friendly Indians with unkempt hair, great eyes and broad cheeks. When the vikings displayed a white shield as a sign of peace, the Indians, who were very timid, fled. They were not seen again that winter, and the small settlement prospered. But in the spring the Indians returned in such large numbers that the estuary 'seemed to be strewn with charcoal'. Soon bartering began, the Indians trading their furs for red cloth and silk. As stocks of cloth began to run out, the vikings cut it into ever smaller pieces until finally they were no bigger than a finger, yet the Indians gave just as much for the cloth as before. They were also eager to obtain weapons, but Karlsefni refused to part with any.

Everything was going well, until the Indians were frightened by a bull. Then one of them who was trying to steal weapons was killed by a viking. These incidents angered the Indians, who left hurriedly. Karlsefni prudently built a stockade around the camp. Three weeks later the Indians launched their expected attack. One of their weapons was a kind of ballista, or catapult. Operated by several men, it hurled a large, dark-coloured ball from the end of a pole. (Research has shown that in the tradition of the Algonquin Indians their forebears used such a weapon, the shot being a boulder sewn into a skin). As the ball fell, it made an awesome noise which so scared the Northmen that they retreated, leaving Thorbrand Snorrison dead. They were rallied by the woman, Freydis, who snatched a sword from the dead man's hand and prepared to defend herself.

When Karlsefni realised that the Indians were hostile he displayed a red shield, hoping that this would indicate his intention to fight. Thereupon the battle began. Two vikings and four Indians were killed before the enemy was driven off.

The tiny colony knew now that they could never hope to be safe from Indian attacks, so they sailed back to Straumfjord where, well-stocked with provisions, they passed their third winter. Thorvald Ericsson, slain by an arrow, was left behind. Nothing went right for them. There were numerous quarrels over women, and when summer came, the whole idea of a settlement in Wineland was abandoned. Karlsefni sailed off in one ship to look for Thorhall the Hunter. Failing to find him, he returned to Straumfjord, and in a second ship set off to Greenland, where he wintered with Eric the Red. Meanwhile, Bjarni Grimolfsson's ship was blown into the Irish Sea where, riddled with worms, it began to sink. Only one boat was serviceable, and as that would take only half the crew, they drew lots for places in it. Bjarni was one of the lucky ones, but he gave up his place to a young Icelander who reproached him with having misled them with unfulfilled promises about Wineland. So Bjarni went down with the ship, scorning death in the true viking way. The boatload of survivors reached Ireland.

In the summer that Karlsefni returned to Greenland, Freydis left her home to visit two brothers, Helgi and Finnbogi, who had recently arrived from Norway in their own ship. They agreed to join her on a Wineland expedition, sharing all profits. Freydis asked her brother, Leif, to give her the houses he had built in Wineland, but he refused, though he offered to lend them to her.

Freydis and the brothers agreed that each party should take thirty able-bodied men, so that neither should have an advantage in numbers, but Freydis smuggled aboard five more. The brothers, with five women in their party, reached Wineland just ahead of Freydis and moved their cargo into Leif's houses. When Freydis arrived, she made them remove their goods, saying that the use of the houses was no part of their agreement. When winter set in, the two parties held games and other entertainments. Then trouble broke out, and all visiting between the two sides ceased.

Early one morning Freydis, bare-footed, visited the brothers' house and suggested that for the sake of peace they might exchange ships, her own being too small for her needs, and that she would then sail away. To this they agreed, and Freydis returned home. Thorvard, her husband, awoke and asked why she was so cold and wet. She told him the brothers had maltreated her when she offered to buy their boat. Then she taunted Thorvard because, she said, he would never avenge her humiliation or his own. Thorvard was at last goaded into avenging the supposed affront. He and his men broke into the brothers' house, and as they and their crew were dragged out, Freydis had them all murdered. As no one was willing to kill the five women, Freydis said, 'Give me an axe,' and she slew them herself.

Freydis thought that she had been very clever to gain possession of their property and threatened her companions with death if they breathed a word of the outrage when they returned to Greenland. They were simply to say, 'these people stayed on when we left'. They reached Greenland in the following spring, and Freydis returned to her farm. She bribed those about her to silence, but the secret leaked out, and when Leif heard of it he seized three of Freydis's men and tortured them until they made a full confession. Leif did not have the heart to punish Freydis, but he prophesied that her descendants would never prosper, and 'after that', continues the saga, 'no one thought anything but ill of her and her family'.

It is related that about 100 years later, Eric Gnupsson, Bishop of Greenland, went in search of Wineland, but no more was heard of him. It is also recorded that a Greenland ship visited Wineland in 1347.

The truth of these accounts has often been disputed by scholars, but details in the sagas of viking settlements in Iceland and Greenland have been verified by archaeologists, and today no one really doubts that vikings reached America. Over the years many searches have been made for evidence of viking

83

occupation, and from time to time claims of such a discovery have been put forward. At the turn of the century, Olf Ohman, a Scandinavian immigrant farmer in Minnesota, which was then peopled by the descendants of Scandinavians and immigrants, announced that from the roots of a yew tree on his wood-lot he had dug a large stone carved with medieval runes. A rune consists of alphabetic symbols used by ancient Teutonic peoples, including Scandinavians. As the stone was found near Kensington, it was known as the Kensington Stone. But it proved to be a forgery, as were four other runic stones, one 'discovered' in Nova Scotia, another in Massachusetts and two in Oklahoma.

Then, in 1957, Laurence Witten, a dealer in rare books in New Haven, Connecticut, produced a world map of AD 1440 which was said to have been drawn by Scandinavian explorers. This is commonly known as the Yale Vinland Map, but doubts have been cast upon its authenticity.

In 1961, after many preliminary surveys, the Norwegians, Helge Ingstad and his wife Anne Stine Ingstad, the archaeological leader of the excavation, began work on a site at L'Anse aux Meadows (Bay of the Meadows), Newfoundland. There, after detailed consideration of all the known facts, it was thought that Leif Ericsson must have beached his ship and made his home. Many searches had previously been made, but nothing had ever been found which could be proved to have been made and used by vikings in America. In 1964 the Ingstads dug up a small soapstone whorl made from a piece of charred cooking-pot. They claimed that this had been used as a flywheel to spin a wooden shaft twisting raw wool into yarn and that it indicated women were with the viking settlers. The expedition also unearthed the turf foundations of nine old structures, the biggest 21 m by 16 m, which was about the right size for a viking great hall. There were also traces of two dwellings about 9 m long, fragments of worked iron and several hundred pieces of slag, which might have been refuse from iron-smelting. As neither

Indians nor Eskimoes in the area knew how to smelt iron, it was claimed that this was evidence of the site being Norse. It was also stated that proof had been obtained by carbon-14 dating that the 'smithy' had been built in viking times.

This method of dating depends upon the fact that all animal and vegetable remains contain a radioactive element of carbon which is termed carbon 14. In most forms of life the proportions are fixed. When a particular form of life dies, the radioactive part of it begins to waste slowly at a known rate, which can be measured. When anything is excavated which contains this element of carbon its age can be calculated to within a few hundred years in many thousands of years. Where the smithy stood, remains were found containing the important element of carbon, and from this the approximate age of the smithy was calculated. Many scholars agreed that it was a viking smithy; others reserved judgement. It is not yet proved beyond all possible doubt that it was indeed a viking smithy, but the broad truth of the landings in America as told in the sagas is generally accepted.

# 9

# HARALD HARDRADA

Harald Sigurdsson, known as Hardrada, the Hard Ruler or the Ruthless, won an unenviable but admired reputation among his fellows for ferocity and vindictiveness. It was said that when his mother, Queen Asa, brought her three sons before King Olaf, who ruled Norway from 1016 to 1030, Olaf scowled at the two older boys until they were almost in tears, but when he scowled at three-year-old Harald, the child merely scowled back. Olaf pulled the boy's hair, and Harald retaliated by tugging the royal moustaches. Olaf laughed and said, 'One day you will be vengeful, kinsman'. On the following day Olaf came upon the boys playing near a lake. Harald was some distance away from the other two, playing with bits of wood on the water, pretending they were warships. Olaf asked the boys in turn what they wanted to be when they grew up. The first wanted as many cornfields as would spread over the ten farms around the lake. The second wanted as many cattle as could stand around the lake shoulder to shoulder when they drank. 'And you?' Olaf addressed Harald. 'I want warriors enough to eat all my brother's cattle in one meal,' Harald answered promptly. 'You will be vengeful when you are a man,' Olaf remarked thoughtfully.

In 1028 Olaf the Stout, as he was called, had been defeated

by a great Anglo-Danish fleet of 1,400 warships led by Canute and had fled to Russia. In 1030, while Canute was in England, Olaf returned by way of Sweden with a scratch army of 2,000 mercenaries to recover Norway. Harald Hardrada, who was his half-brother, accompanied him. Olaf decided to open his campaign by crushing the nobles and peasants of the district of Trondelag, and chose Stiklestad as the site to fight on. The battle was the first in the history of Norway to have been fought on land. Just before it began, Olaf suggested that Harald should not take part in it as he was too young. Harald was then fifteen; a Scandinavian boy was considered to have reached manhood at the age of twelve. 'If I am too weak to grasp my sword, I shall tie my hand to its hilt,' declared Harald. 'I mean to be with my men.'

Olaf fell under his banner, struck down by sword, spear and axe. After this, Olaf the Stout became Olaf the Saint, for the church considered that a saint would strengthen its hold in Norway.

Harald was wounded, but was smuggled away to a lonely farmhouse in the forest where he was cared for until his wounds were healed. Then, keeping to forest tracks for safety, he made his way over the mountains to Sweden where many of Olaf's men joined him. In the spring Harald collected several ships. Crossing the sea, he led his followers to the court of King Jaroslav, prince of Kiev. Harald was single-minded in his determination to win power and revenge, and he needed money. He stayed the winter with Jaroslav who appointed him a commander in the Varangian Guard, and he fought against both Slavs and Poles, gathering much plunder in the process. His rapacity was too much for Jaroslav who persuaded him to sell his sword elsewhere. With 500 warriors behind him, Harald entered the service of the emperor of Constantinople. He campaigned in Palestine and even threatened Jerusalem. Then he was sent to Sicily where the emperor's army was campaigning against the Arabs.

A saga tells of the ingenious but cruel way Harald dealt with a Sicilian town whose walls were too strong for him to break. He ordered bird-catchers to collect a large number of small birds. Their wings were smeared with wax and sulphur, to which wood shavings were stuck. The shavings were set alight and the birds released, whereupon they flew to their nests in the town, setting fire to the thatched roofs above them, and soon the whole town was ablaze.

The Empress Zoe was a woman of Harald's mould. She had arranged for her first husband to be murdered in his bath. Her second husband, joint ruler with her, was the Emperor Michael Calaphates. It was not long before Zoe had Harald seized for alleged thefts from the royal treasury. He was clapped in a dungeon but escaped. There was a palace revolution, and the emperor fled from a furious mob and sought refuge in a monastery disguised as a monk. He was tracked down by the Varangian Guard, and Harald, at a prefect's bidding, put out his eyes.

Harald prudently left Constantinople, sailing off with two ships and abducting the emperor's niece, Maria, on the way. Chains across the Bosphorus barred his exit. By putting all the weight on the stern of his ship, he tilted the prow until it was over the chains, then he ordered everyone forward, and his ship slid to safety. The companion vessel, however, broke its back on the chain and sank, drowning several of its crew. Harald put Maria ashore, and then made his way back to Jaroslav under whom he re-enlisted. Later he married Elizabeth, Jaroslav's daughter, and collected the vast treasure with which he could buy all the ships and men he needed. Returning to Norway, he used it as a base for attacks upon Denmark, which he plundered mercilessly time and again, carrying many women into slavery.

King Magnus, his nephew, gave him a half share of Norway in return for half his plunder, and when Magnus died, Harald became sole ruler. He mobilised half his ships and men and plundered Jutland. Then he married for the second time. Every summer he plundered Denmark; among the towns he destroyed by fire was Hedeby, the great trading centre.

Gentleness was foreign to his nature. When farmers protested against taxes and other dues, he dealt with them brutally. One poet commented, 'Flames cured the peasants of disloyalty to Harald'. For twenty years he ruled Norway with an iron hand, crushing all opposition and murdering possible rivals.

Now his ambitions turned to England where there had been trouble and unrest after the death of Canute in 1035. Harold Harefoot, Canute's son by an English mother, succeeded him and died unlamented after a short reign of five years. Hardicanute, King of Denmark, obtained the English crown but lost his Danish throne in doing so; he, too, soon died. Edward, Aethelred's only surviving son, then became king of England, thus ending Danish rule. When he died, Earl Godwin's son, Harold, claimed the throne. He had been Edward's chief minister for thirteen years, and said that Edward had promised him the succession. But William, seventh Duke of Normandy, a descendant of the viking Duke Rollo, maintained that he was the rightful successor to the throne of England and that Harold had sworn allegiance to him over holy relics.

Harold's brother, Tostig, a violent man whom Harold had exiled, also schemed against him and attacked the English coast, but was repelled by the Earl of Mercia. Tostig sheltered temporarily with King Malcolm of Scotland, then sailed to Norway to enlist Harald's support. Finding himself unwelcome, Tostig looted, burned and slew before returning to England with the intention of winning Harold's throne, but abandoned the idea when his fleet was reduced to only twelve ships. Once more he visited Scotland in a fruitless attempt to enlist Malcolm's aid, and then yet again sailed to Norway. On this occasion he persuaded Harald that the English throne was his for the taking and that Malcolm would be their ally.

Harald's fleet assembled in the Solund Islands. Before sailing for England, he opened St Olaf's shrine in Trondheim. To propitiate his spirit, he trimmed the saint's hair and nails, after which he locked the shrine and threw the key into the river Nid. Harald had his son, Magnus, proclaimed king and left him in Norway as his regent. Then, accompanied by his wife and their daughters, Maria and Ingigerd, Harald sailed across the North Sea in a boat made at Trondheim. 'Much broader than the normal warships, and the same size and proportion as the *Long Serpent*,' says *King Harald's Saga*, 'its prow had a dragon's head, the stern had a dragon's tail, and the bows were inlaid with gold.' He made a landfall at Orkney where he gathered large reinforcements before sailing further south.

After a vain attempt to win Malcolm's assistance, Tostig sailed to his rendezvous with Harald in the river Tyne. The combined viking fleet landed at Cleveland on the Yorkshire coast and began plundering. After ravaging the countryside, they sailed on to Scarborough and fought with the townsmen. Lighted faggots were hurled from the top of a rock on to the thatched roofs of some houses, and soon the town was ablaze, pillaged and razed to the ground.

Messengers posted south to Harold with the bad news, a journey of several days. William of Normandy's own attack had begun and his fleet had already made contact with the English fleet, though the engagement was broken off by the Normans because of a storm. It was at this time that Harold heard that Harald and Tostig were preparing to attack York and, though he made a forced march, he was too late to save it. Harald had landed at Riccall on the river Ouse, ten miles south of York, had broken Earl Morcar's army, slain the earl and seized the city.

Harald was warned of the English approach and set off to meet them, but he did not know their strength nor that Harold was with them. Harold's march had been held up for a time by an enormous viking who had straddled a bridge and slain forty men with his axe before an Englishman paddled a swill-tub under the bridge and speared him through a gap in the planks.

It was 29 September 1066, and Harold had marched 190 miles from London in five days. It was a hot day, and most of the vikings had discarded their sweltering *byrnies*, the knee-length leather coats sewn with iron rings and studs. Harald, too, had thrown off his coat, *Emma*. He ignored Tostig's warning against marching without body armour, and only a hundred or so of his men were properly armed. Not expecting a battle, he led his men to Stamford Bridge where he was shocked to see fluttering in the wind the golden dragon banner of Wessex and Harold's personal banner, the Fighting Man, woven in thread of gold. The English weapons 'sparkled like a field of broken ice'.

When the two armies drew together, Harold tried to conciliate his brother Tostig by offering to return his forfeited earldom and make him joint ruler over one-third of the kingdom. Tostig refused, and asked what he proposed to offer King Harald Sigurdsson. 'Six feet of ground or as much more than he is taller than other men,' Harold answered him.

Harald wore a blue tunic and a splendid helmet. He was 51 years old, very tall and handsome, with a fair beard and long moustache. His face bore the scar of an old wound and one eyebrow was slightly higher than the other.

Harold had 20,000 men, Harald only half that number. At the third attack Harald fell with an arrow in his throat. The wound was mortal. When he heard of it, Harold again offered Tostig peace, and again it was refused. Then Tostig, too, was slain by an arrow. The vikings received reinforcements led by the Orkney earls. The newcomers had marched fast; the men were in full armour and near exhaustion. To fight more freely they, too, made the fatal mistake of throwing off their *byrnies*. Their resistance was soon broken, and when darkness fell only scattered knots of vikings were still fighting. A week after the battle, Harold had to hurry south to confront William of Normandy, and at Senlac, among the bodies of his faithful housecarls and his Wessex thanes, he, too, fell.

Of the 300 ships of the viking invasion fleet, only twenty-four, led by Olaf Haraldsson, were needed to repatriate the sad survivors. With them, on its last dark voyage, went the body of Harald Hardrada, the most famous viking of his day. When this poor remnant of the fleet reached Orkney, the vikings learned that Harald's daughter, Maria, had died at the same hour as her father. Losing all heart to return to Norway, they settled at Bersay under the protection of the Orkney earls.

The Northmen's 350 years of harassment of Britain were at last ended, and the Viking Age drew to its close.

# BIBLIOGRAPHY

Brøndsted, Johannes. *The Vikings* (1960; reprint 1971)

Bryant, Arthur. *The Story of England* (1953)

Butler, Dennis. *The Story of a Year* (1966)

Churchill, Winston. *The History of the English-Speaking Peoples*, vol I (1956)

Davidson, H. R. Ellis. *Gods and Myths of Northern Europe* (1964; reprint 1972)

Foote, P. G. and Wilson, D. M. *The Viking Achievement* (1970)

Larsen, Sofas. *The Discovery of North America Twenty Years Before Columbus* (Copenhagen 1925)

Magnusson, Magnus and Palsson, Hermann (trans). *The Vinland Sagas*

Magnusson, Magnus and Palsson, Hermann (trans). *King Harald's Saga*

Magnusson, Magnus and Palsson, Hermann (trans). *Njal's Saga*

Sturluson, Snorri. *Heimskringla*, vols 717, 847 (Everyman's Library 1930)

Wainwright, F. T. (ed). *The Northern Isles* (1962)

Whitelock, Dorothy (ed). *The Anglo-Saxon Chronicle* (1961)

# ACKNOWLEDGEMENTS

Thanks are due to the following for permission to reproduce the photographs: British Museum, pages 8, 16, 18 (right), 19 (top), 52, 56; Museum of National Antiquities, Stockholm, 18 (centre), 23, 24, 26, 29, 31 (right), 33, 44, 47, 54, 65; National Museum, Copenhagen, 2 (bottom), 17, 19 (bottom), 20, 22, 25, 34, 36; National Museum, Reykjavik, 31 (left); National Museum of Antiquities, Scotland, 21; Osterreichische National-bibliothek, 77; Universitetets Oldsaksamling, Oslo, 2 (top), 15, 16 (bottom), 18 (left), 21 (left), 27, 37, 38, 39, 40, 41, 42, 43.

# INDEX

Page numbers in italics indicate illustrations.

95